PATRIOTISM ON CELLULOID

AN EXPLORATION OF INDIA'S INSPIRING FILMS

DR. JAGADEESH PILLAI

‖ Dedicated to all Indian Youngsters Around The World ‖

Contents

Contents

Prayer

"Om Asato Maa Sadgamaya,Tamaso Maa Jyotir Gamaya,Mrityor Maa Amritam Gamaya, Om Shantih, Shantih, Shantih"

The true meaning of this mantra is: OM guide me from the unreal to the real, from darkness to light, and from mortality to immortality.
OM Peace, Peace, Peace.

About The Author

Dr. Jagadeesh Pillai is a renowned Guinness World Record holder, writer, and researcher hailing from Varanasi, also known as the abode of Lord Shiva. With a Ph.D. in Vedic Science and a range of creative ideas and achievements, he is a true polymath. He is the author of more than 100 books including Research Publications. Although his roots can be traced back to Kerala, the people of Varanasi hold him in high regard and affectionately consider him one of their own.

Dr. Pillai has achieved four Guinness World Records in the following subjects:

1. "Script to Screen" - In this record, Dr. Pillai produced and directed an animation film within the shortest time possible, breaking the previous record set by Canadians. He has also received numerous national and international awards and recognitions for this achievement.

2. Longest Line of Postcards - For this record, Dr. Pillai created a line of 16,300 postcards on the occasion of the 163rd anniversary of Indian Postal Day. The event also included a questionnaire about the Indian flag.

3. Largest Poster Awareness Campaign - Dr. Pillai designed an awareness campaign on the subject of "Beti Bachao - Beti Padhao" (Save the Girl Child - Educate the Girl Child) to achieve this record.

4. Largest Envelope - In tribute to the Indian Prime Minister's "Make in India" initiative, Dr. Pillai created a 4000 square meter envelope using waste paper to achieve this record.

5. Attempted - 70000 Candles on a 210 kg Cake - To celebrate the 70th Indian Independence Day, Dr. Pillai attempted to light 70,000 candles on a 210 kg cake, which was recorded in World Records India.

6. Attempted - Documentary on Dhamek Stupa of Sarnath in 17 Languages - Dr. Pillai attempted to create a documentary on the Dhamek Stupa of Sarnath, dubbing it in 17 different languages. The result of this attempt is currently awaiting confirmation from the Guinness World Records.

Dr. Pillai is skilled in teaching the Bhagavad Gita, a Hindu scripture, and is popular among young people. He has helped many young people improve their lives through his motivational teachings.

In addition to teaching, he has composed and sung numerous Sanskrit Bhajans and patriotic songs.

He has also written and directed several short films and documentaries for awareness campaigns, and has volunteered with the police in both UP and Kerala to spread awareness about various issues through videos and photography.

He has a goal of writing thousands of books on Indian culture, Indian temples, and the lives of extraordinary people. Incredibly, he has produced and directed over 100 documentaries about the city of Varanasi, all on his own.

He has also helped and guided more than 25 boys and girls to achieve world records through creative and innovative methods. He is a multifaceted person who uses his intellect and the blessings given to him by God to excel in various areas. He is both a teacher and a student, always learning and teaching, and is able to master any subject he comes across.

He is a selfless social activist and motivational speaker who has overcome struggles and failures to become a successful and enthusiastic individual with a rich life experience.

In addition to his work with the Bhagavad Gita, he is also an efficient Tarot card reader, Astro-Vastu consultant, and a talented singer and composer. He has sung the entire Ram Charita Manas and Bhagavad Gita in his own compositions, and has sung the phrase "Lokah Samastha Sukhino Bhavantu" in 50 different languages. He is currently working on a detailed and scientific study of Vedas, Upanishads, Puranas, and the Bhagavad Gita. He has also composed and sung the Hanuman Chalisa and Gayatri Mantra in 108 and 1008 different compositions, respectively.

Awards - Four Times Guinness World Records, Winner of Mahatma Gandhi Vishwa Shanti Puraskar , Mahatma Gandhi Global Peace Ambassador, Kashi Ratna Award, Dr. APJ Abdul Kalam Motivational Person of the Year 2017, Mother Teresa Award, Indira Gandhi Priyadarshini Award, Bharat Vikas Ratna Award, Udyog Ratna Award, Vigyan Prasar Award, Poorvanchal Ratn Samman.

Preface

Patriotic films have always played an important role in shaping the cultural and political landscape of India. These films, with their powerful stories and messages, have the ability to inspire and motivate audiences to take action for the betterment of their country. This book "Patriotic Films" is a collection of brief summaries of some of the most impactful patriotic films to come out of India, with a focus on the patriotism depicted in each film.

The films discussed in this book range from historical dramas to biographical films and cover a wide range of themes and subjects, from the struggles for freedom and independence to the impact of socio-economic issues on the nation. Each film is presented in a concise and easy-to-digest format, providing readers with a quick reference guide to the patriotism depicted in each film.

The films covered in this book are not only entertaining but also provide a window into the rich cultural and political history of India. They showcase the resilience and determination of the Indian people in the face of adversity, and their unyielding spirit to achieve freedom and independence. From the pioneering spirit of the team behind the first Indian feature film "Harishchandrachi Factory" to the powerful depiction of Mahatma Gandhi's non-violent resistance movement in "Gandhi" and "Gandhi, My Father", these films remind us of the sacrifices made by those who fought for India's freedom and inspire us to continue their legacy.

The films discussed in this book also highlight the importance of education and self-reliance as powerful tools for change, as seen in the film "I am Kalam", it shows how even the poorest and most marginalized individuals can achieve greatness through hard work and dedication. They also serve as a reminder of the destructive consequences of religious extremism and the need for tolerance and unity, as seen in "Hey Ram".

This book is a must-read for anyone interested in Indian cinema and the rich cultural and political history of India. It provides a quick reference guide to some of the most impactful patriotic films, and the patriotism depicted in each film, which will not only entertain but also educate and inspire readers to take action for the betterment of their country. This book is dedicated to all the patriotic film makers who have played a vital role in shaping the nation's consciousness.

Haqeeqat

"Haqeeqat" is a war film that depicts the heroism and sacrifice of Indian soldiers during the 1962 Sino-Indian War. The film showcases the patriotism and selflessness of the soldiers who fought to defend their country, and the impact of their sacrifices on the families they left behind.

Border

"Border" is another war film, set during the 1971 Indo-Pakistani War. The film depicts the bravery and patriotism of Indian soldiers who fought to defend their country against the Pakistani army. The film's portrayal of the soldiers' unwavering devotion to their country and their sacrifices had a significant impact on the audience and reinforced the idea of love and respect towards the country.

CHAPTER THREE

Mother India

"Mother India" is a 1957 classic film that depicts the struggles of rural Indian farmers, who despite facing difficult living conditions, remain fiercely patriotic and determined to build a better future for their country. The film celebrated the resilience and patriotism of the Indian people, and it had a profound impact on the Indian psyche, serving as a source of inspiration for future generations.

CHAPTER FOUR

Rang De Basanti

"Rang De Basanti" is a 2006 film that depicts a group of young friends who are inspired to take action against the government's corruption and inefficiency. The film explores the idea of patriotism and how it can evolve and take on different forms, particularly with the youth. The film was well-received and praised for its ability to convey the importance of taking action to improve one's country and the impact it had on the youth of the country.

CHAPTER FIVE

Chak De India

"Chak De India" is a 2007 film that tells the story of a former hockey player who takes on the challenge of coaching the Indian women's hockey team to victory. The film is a story of redemption, perseverance, and patriotism. The team, made up of players from different backgrounds and religions, overcomes their differences to come together and represent their country on the global stage. Through their journey, they not only become champions but they also become a symbol of unity and national pride. The film's portrayal of teamwork and national unity had a significant impact on the audience and reinforced the idea of working together for a common goal.

CHAPTER SIX

Lagaan

"Lagaan" is a 2001 film set in British colonial India, that tells the story of a group of farmers who come together to play a game of cricket against the British officers in order to avoid paying high taxes. The film is a story of perseverance and determination, and how the love for one's country can inspire people to achieve the impossible. The film's portrayal of the struggles of farmers and how they were willing to put everything on the line for the sake of their country had a profound impact on the audience and served as a source of inspiration for future generations.

CHAPTER SEVEN

Bhaag Milkha Bhaag

"Bhaag Milkha Bhaag" is a 2013 film based on the true story of Milkha Singh, a former Indian athlete who overcame his personal demons to become one of India's most successful athletes. The film is a story of perseverance, sacrifice, and patriotism. Through Milkha's journey, the audience is reminded of the sacrifices and hard work it takes to become a champion, and how the love for one's country can inspire and motivate individuals to achieve their dreams.

CHAPTER EIGHT

Swades

"Swades" is a 2004 film that tells the story of a successful Indian-American NASA engineer who returns to India to find his roots and reconnect with his country. The film is a story of personal growth, responsibility and patriotism. Through his journey, the character realized the importance of giving back to his country and how the love for one's country can inspire and motivate individuals to make a difference. The film was well-received and praised for its ability to convey the message of patriotism and responsibility towards the country.

Uri

"Uri: The Surgical Strike" is a 2019 film that is based on the real-life events of the surgical strikes carried out by the Indian army in 2016, in response to a terrorist attack on an army base in Uri, Jammu and Kashmir. The film is a story of bravery, sacrifice and patriotism, depicting how the Indian army, with precision and determination, conducted the strikes and successfully avenged the attack. The film's portrayal of the Indian army's heroism and their unwavering devotion to their country had a significant impact on the audience and reinforced the idea of love and respect towards the country and it's army.

CHAPTER TEN

The Kargil War

"The Kargil War" is a 1999 film based on the Kargil War that took place between India and Pakistan. The film depicts the heroism and patriotism of Indian soldiers who fought to defend their country against the Pakistani army. The film's portrayal of the soldiers' unwavering devotion to their country and their sacrifices had a significant impact on the audience and reinforced the idea of love and respect towards the country and it's army.

CHAPTER ELEVEN

The Accidental Prime Minister

"The Accidental Prime Minister" is a 2019 film that depicts the story of former Indian Prime Minister Dr. Manmohan Singh and his tenure in office. The film is a political drama and showcases how politics can affect a leader's decision making and how hard it is to govern a country. The film may have caused some controversies, however, it underlines the level of dedication and patriotism that politicians have towards their country and how it can drive their decision making.

CHAPTER TWELVE

Parmanu

"Parmanu: The Story of Pokhran" is a 2018 film that tells the story of the 1998 Indian nuclear tests in Pokhran. The film is a story of perseverance, sacrifice, and patriotism. It portrays the dedication and commitment of a group of scientists and government officials to make India a nuclear power, despite the many obstacles they faced. The film's portrayal of India's journey to become a nuclear power and the sacrifices made by the scientists and government officials had a significant impact on the audience, and reinforced the idea of love and respect towards the country.

CHAPTER THIRTEEN

Gandhi

"Gandhi" is a 1982 film that depicts the life of Mahatma Gandhi and his non-violent movement to bring about Indian independence from British rule directed by Richard Attenborough. The film is a story of perseverance, sacrifice, and patriotism, showcasing how one man's unwavering commitment to non-violence and his love for his country could inspire a nation to fight for their freedom. The film's portrayal of Gandhi's leadership and the impact of his non-violent movement had a significant impact on the audience, and reinforced the idea of love and respect towards the country.

CHAPTER FOURTEEN

Mughal-e-Azam

"Mughal-e-Azam" is a 1960 film which was one of the biggest blockbuster of its time, is a historical drama that tells the story of the Mughal Prince Salim and his love for the court dancer Anarkali. The film is a story of love, sacrifice, and patriotism, depicting how the love for one's country can inspire individuals to make the ultimate sacrifice for the greater good. The film's portrayal of the sacrifices made by the characters and their unwavering devotion to their country had a profound impact on the audience, and served as a source of inspiration for future generations.

CHAPTER FIFTEEN

Shaheed

"Shaheed" (1965 film) is a film based on the life of Bhagat Singh, one of India's most iconic freedom fighters. The film is a story of sacrifice and patriotism, depicting how one man's unwavering commitment to his country and his willingness to make the ultimate sacrifice, can inspire a nation to fight for their freedom. The film's portrayal of Bhagat Singh's heroism and the impact of his sacrifice had a significant impact on the audience and reinforced the idea of love and respect towards the country.

CHAPTER SIXTEEN

Tirangaa

"Tirangaa" is a 1992 film is a patriotic drama film that tells the story of a patriotic retired army officer who decides to protect his country from terrorists. The film is a story of bravery, sacrifice, and patriotism, depicting how the love for one's country can inspire individuals to put their lives on the line to protect their country. The film's portrayal of the protagonist's heroism and the sacrifices he makes for his country had a significant impact on the audience, and reinforced the idea of love and respect towards the country.

CHAPTER SEVENTEEN

The Legend of Bhagat Singh

"The Legend of Bhagat Singh" is a 2002 film that is based on the life of Bhagat Singh, one of India's most iconic freedom fighters. The film is a story of sacrifice and patriotism, depicting how one man's unwavering commitment to his country and his willingness to make the ultimate sacrifice, can inspire a nation to fight for their freedom. The film's portrayal of Bhagat Singh's life, his beliefs, and the impact of his sacrifice had a significant impact on the audience, and reinforced the idea of love and respect towards the country.

CHAPTER EIGHTEEN

Mangal Pandey: The Rising

"Mangal Pandey: The Rising" is a 2005 film based on the life of Mangal Pandey, a soldier in the British Indian army who was one of the key figures in the Indian Rebellion of 1857. The film is a story of sacrifice and patriotism, depicting how one man's willingness to stand up against the oppression of the British and his love for his country can inspire others to do the same. The film's portrayal of Pandey's life, beliefs and his sacrifice had a significant impact on the audience, and reinforced the idea of love and respect towards the country.

Netaji Subhas Chandra Bose

"Netaji Subhas Chandra Bose: The Forgotten Hero" is a 2005 film based on the life of Subhas Chandra Bose, an Indian nationalist who is remembered for his contributions in the Indian independence movement. The film is a story of sacrifice and patriotism, depicting how one man's unwavering commitment to his country and his willingness to make the ultimate sacrifice can inspire a nation to fight for their freedom. The film's portrayal of Bose's life, his beliefs and the impact of his sacrifice had a significant impact on the audience and reinforced the idea of love and respect towards the country.

CHAPTER TWENTY

Roar of the Lion

"Roar of the Lion" is a 2019 documentary film that chronicles the Indian cricket team's journey to win the 2019 Cricket World Cup. The film showcases the team's perseverance, sacrifice, and patriotism, as they overcame several obstacles to win the tournament. The film's portrayal of the team's journey and the impact of their victory had a significant impact on the audience and reinforced the idea of love and respect towards the country.

CHAPTER TWENTY-ONE

Pareeksha

"Pareeksha" is a 2020 film that is based on the true story of a rickshaw driver who wants to provide a better education for his son, so he can have a better life. The film is a story of perseverance, sacrifice, and patriotism, depicting how the love for one's country can inspire individuals to make a difference in their community. The film's portrayal of the protagonist's struggles and his unwavering devotion to his country had a significant impact on the audience and reinforced the idea of love and respect towards the country.

CHAPTER TWENTY-TWO

Satyagraha

"Satyagraha" is a 2013 film that is a political drama that depicts how individuals from different backgrounds come together to fight against corruption and bring about political change in their country. The film is a story of perseverance, sacrifice, and patriotism, depicting how the love for one's country can inspire individuals to make a difference. The film's portrayal of the characters' struggles and their unwavering devotion to their country had a significant impact on the audience and reinforced the idea of love and respect towards the country.

CHAPTER TWENTY-THREE

Purab Aur Paschim

"Purab Aur Paschim" is a 1970 film which is a classic and shows the contrasts between the traditional and modern ways of living of the people of India. It also tells the story of a man who goes to America to find success but eventually returns to India, to find true happiness and meaning in his life. The film's portrayal of the characters' struggles and their unwavering devotion to their country had a significant impact on the audience and reinforced the idea of love and respect towards the country and how true happiness comes from being connected with the nation and its culture.

CHAPTER TWENTY-FOUR

The Black Prince

"The Black Prince" is a 2017 film that tells the story of the last king of Punjab, Maharaja Duleep Singh and his relationship with Queen Victoria. The film portrays the king's struggles to come to terms with his identity and his relationship with his homeland, and how ultimately his love for his country and people led him to fight for their rights. The film's portrayal of Duleep Singh's life, struggles, and his unwavering devotion to his country and people had a significant impact on the audience and reinforced the idea of love and respect towards the country.

CHAPTER TWENTY-FIVE

The Attack of 26/11

"The Attack of 26/11" is a 2013 film that is based on the 2008 terrorist attacks in Mumbai, India. The film is a story of bravery and sacrifice, depicting how the Mumbai police force, along with the Indian army, worked tirelessly to end the terrorist siege and protect the city's citizens. The film's portrayal of the sacrifices made by the security forces and their unwavering devotion to their country had a significant impact on the audience, and reinforced the idea of love and respect towards the country.

CHAPTER TWENTY-SIX

Prithvi

"Prithvi" is a 1997 film based on the life of Indian freedom fighter Prithvi Singh Azad, who fought against British colonial rule. The film is a story of sacrifice and patriotism, depicting how one man's unwavering commitment to his country and his willingness to make the ultimate sacrifice can inspire a nation to fight for their freedom. The film's portrayal of Prithvi Singh's life, his beliefs, and the impact of his sacrifice had a significant impact on the audience, and reinforced the idea of love and respect towards the country.

CHAPTER TWENTY-SEVEN

My Birthday Song

"My Birthday Song" although it is not primarily a patriotic film, however, it has a subtle undertone of nationalism feeling, which is portrayed through the protagonist's personal growth journey, as he comes to accept and own his past, learning to be proud of his heritage and finally taking a stand for himself and his family against the forces of evil. In a way, the film showcases how by being true to oneself and one's beliefs, one can contribute to the larger good of the nation.

CHAPTER TWENTY-EIGHT

Mission Mangal

"Mission Mangal" is a film that showcases the immense patriotism shown by the team of scientists at the Indian Space Research Organisation (ISRO) as they work towards the successful launch of India's first interplanetary mission, the Mars Orbiter Mission. The film portrays the struggles, setbacks, and eventual triumph of the team, in their relentless pursuit of excellence, a spirit of perseverance, and a deep-rooted desire to make India proud. It is a true celebration of the team's undying spirit and the relentless pursuit of excellence, which is the very embodiment of the patriotic sentiment that drives a nation towards greatness. The film showcases a strong sense of national pride and the indomitable spirit of a team of brilliant scientists, as they work towards a common goal, that of putting India on the map of space exploration.

CHAPTER TWENTY-NINE

Am Kalam

"I Am Kalam" is a 2011 Indian drama film directed by Nila Madhab Panda. The film tells the story of a poor boy named Chhotu who is inspired by the former President of India, A. P. J. Abdul Kalam, and sets out to become like him. The film is a powerful tribute to the spirit of self-reliance and the power of education to break the cycle of poverty. It also showcases the patriotism through the character's admiration of the Indian President and his determination to become like him, which symbolizes the desire of the common man to become an agent of change in the nation.

CHAPTER THIRTY

Hey Ram

"Hey Ram" is a 2000 Indian crime period drama film simultaneously made in Hindi and Tamil languages. Written and directed by Kamal Haasan, The film explores the assassination of Mahatma Gandhi from the perspective of a Hindu nationalist who eventually becomes disillusioned with the politics of hatred and violence. The film showcases the patriotism and love for the country but also highlights the destructive consequences of religious extremism and the need for tolerance and unity. The film is a powerful commentary on the need to reject hatred and violence in favor of reconciliation and understanding, as the only way to achieve true patriotism and national unity.

Harishchandrachi Factory

"Harishchandrachi Factory" is a 2009 Indian Marathi-language biographical film directed by Paresh Mokashi. The film tells the story of the making of the first Indian feature film, Raja Harishchandra, directed by Dadasaheb Phalke and released in 1913. The film is a tribute to the pioneering spirit of Phalke and his team, and their contribution to the birth of Indian cinema. The film also showcases a strong sense of patriotism as it tells the story of the first Indian feature film and the hard work and dedication put in by its team to bring it to life, which symbolizes the indomitable spirit of the Indian people to excel and make their mark in the world.

CHAPTER THIRTY-TWO

Half Ticket

"Half Ticket" is a 1962 Indian Hindi-language film directed by Kalidas. The film is a comedy about two street urchins who sneak into a movie theater using a half-ticket. The film's humor and light-hearted tone belie its underlying message of the power of imagination and the ability of even the most downtrodden to dream and aspire. The film reflects the patriotism as it shows how even the less privileged children, who cannot afford a full ticket, want to experience and be a part of the Indian cinema, which symbolizes the resilience and the desire of the common man to be a part of the nation's cultural and artistic landscape.

CHAPTER THIRTY-THREE

Gandhi, My Father

"Gandhi, My Father" is a 2007 Indian biographical drama film directed by Feroz Abbas Khan. The film tells the story of the troubled relationship between Mahatma Gandhi and his eldest son, Harilal Gandhi. The film is a powerful exploration of the human side of one of the greatest figures of the 20th century, and an examination of the sacrifices made by those who strive for freedom and justice. The film reflects a strong sense of patriotism through the portrayal of the life and struggles of Mahatma Gandhi, who is considered as one of the most prominent figures in Indian history, who's ideologies and principles led India to freedom and also showcases the emotional and personal cost of his actions, which serves as a reminder of the sacrifices made by those who fought for India's freedom.

Chittagong

"Chittagong" is a 2012 Indian historical drama film directed by Bedabrata Pain. The film tells the story of the Chittagong Uprising, an armed rebellion led by a group of schoolboys against the British Raj in India in 1930. The film showcases a strong sense of patriotism as it tells the story of the Chittagong Uprising, which was one of the earliest forms of armed resistance against the British Raj and also highlights the sacrifices made by the young revolutionary who were determined to fight for India's freedom. The film is a powerful tribute to the spirit of resistance and the courage of those who fought against the oppressive forces of colonialism.

CHAPTER THIRTY-FIVE

SUMMARY

All these films depict the various forms of patriotism and how it can inspire and motivate individuals to strive for a better country. These films serve as a reminder of the sacrifices made by freedom fighters, sportspersons and the common man and the importance of working together for a common goal of success, a better future and education for the country. They also showcase how patriotism can be expressed in various ways, through personal struggles, sacrifices and finding meaning and happiness in the nation and its culture.

Other Books Of The Author

1. The Moments When I Met God
2. Kashiyile Theertha Pathangal
3. GURU GYAN VANI
4. Abhiprerak Gita
5. ASSI SE JAIN GHAT TAK
6. Hopelessness of Arjuna
7. The Soul and It's True Nature
8. Sense of Action (Karma)
9. Action through Wisdom
10. Action through Wisdom
11. THEORY AND PRACTICAL OF EVERY ACTION
12. LOGICAL UNDERSTANDING OF THE SUPREME
13. THE IMPERISHABLE SUPREME
14. Yatra Nishadraj se Hanuman Ghat Tak
15. Yatra Karnatak Ghat se Raja Ghat Tak
16. Yatra Pandey Ghat se Prayagraj Ghat Tak
17. Yatra Ranjendra Prasad Ghat se Dattatreya Ghat Tak
18. YaatraSindhiya Ghat se Gwaliar Ghat Tak
19. Yatra Mangala Gauri Ghat se Hanuman Gadhi Ghat Tak
20. Yatra Gaay Ghat Se Nishad Ghat Tak
21. MAA GANGA, GHATEN EVM UTSAV
22. Ganga Arti Dev Deepavali evam Any Utsav
23. Potentials of Digitalized India
24. VEDIC CONSCIOUSNESS
25. A Brief Introduction to Vedic Science
26. Kashi ke Barah Jyotirling
27. IMPACT OF MOTIVATION
28. Let's have a Milky Way Journey
29. Color Therapy in a Nutshell

30. Rigveda in a Nutshell
31. Yajurveda in a Nutshell
32. Samveda in a Nutshell
33. Atharva Veda in a Nutshell
34. Ayushman Bhava - Ayurveda
35. Srimad Bhagavad Gita and Upanishad Connection
36. Srimad Bhagavad Gita - an attempt to summarize each chapter
37. Facts and Impact of Nakshatra
38. Astro Gems - NAVARATNA
39. Ekadashi - A Concise Overview
40. A Concise View of Hanuman Chalisa
41. Inspirational Gita
42. Nakshatraranyam
43. Summary of 18 Mahapuranas
44. Synopsis of 18 Upa Puranas
45. Rigvediya Upanishads
46. Shukla Yajurvediya Upanishads
47. Krishna Yajurvediya Upanishads
48. Samavediya Upanishads
49. Atharvavediya Upanishads
50. The Seven Great Sages
51. From Rocket Scientist to President Dr. APJ Abdul Kalam
52. The Visionary's Voice - Quotes of Dr. APJ Abdul Kalam
53. The Wisdom of Swami Vivekananda.
54. Ayurvedic Remedies from the Garden
55. Sages and Seers
56. Rising Strong – Motivational Stories of Women
57. Beyond Flames -Mystery stories of Funeral Ghat Manikarnika
58. The Origins of Tulsi: A Look at the Mythological Roots of the Plant
59. The Holistic Cow

60. Arts of Healing
61. Exploring the Divine
62. Understanding Five Elements
63. The Etymology of Ram
64. Symbols of India
65. Voice of Change (About Speeches of Great Men)
66. She Speaks (About Speeches of Great Men)

Contact

DR. JAGADEESH PILLAI

PhD in Vedic Science

Four Times Guinness World Record Holder

Winner of Mahatma Gandhi Vishwa Shanti Puraskar and
Global Peace Ambassador

Gemology, Astro & Vastu Consultant - Spiritual Counselor

Consultant for designing World Record Ideas

Efficient Tarot Card Reader

9839093003

myrichindia@gmail.com

drjagadeeshpillai@facebook

drjagadeeshpillai@instagram

jagadeeshpillai@youtube

www. JAGADEESHPILLAI.com

|| LOKAHA SAMASTHAHA SUKHINO BHAVANTU ||

www.ingramcontent.com/pod-product-compliance
Lightning Source LLC
Chambersburg PA
CBHW031242130726
47988CB00008B/3203